KS2
Success
Revision Guide

Lynn Huggins-Cooper

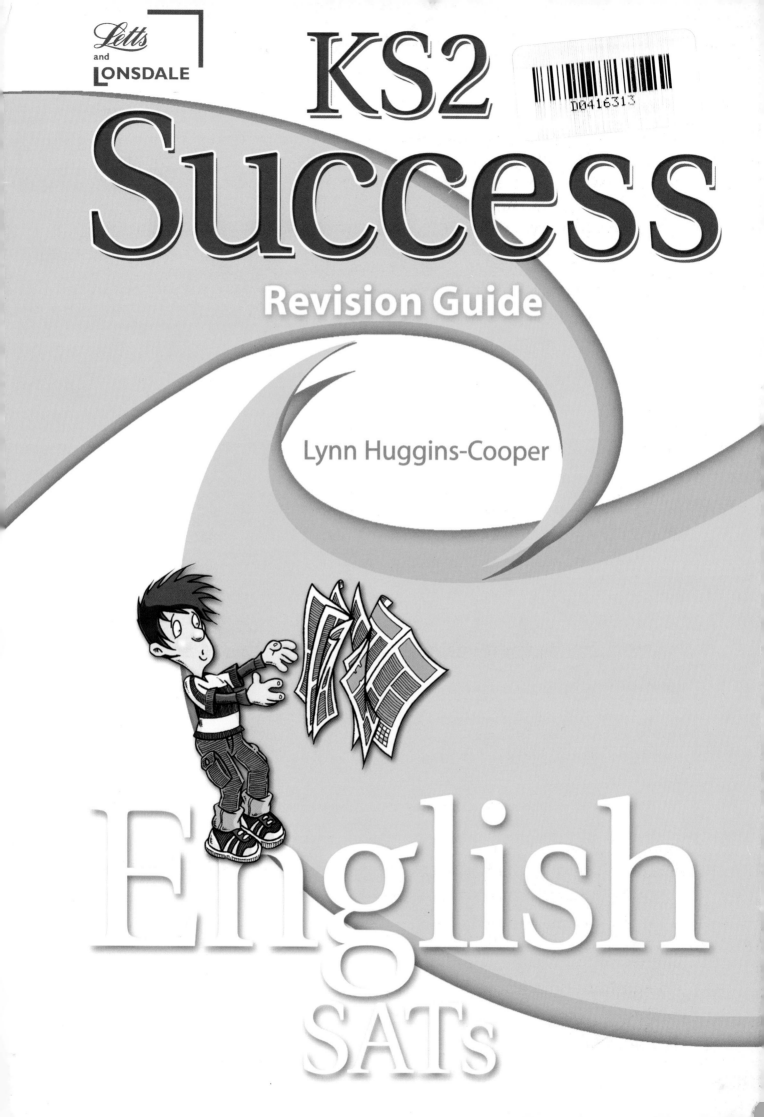

English
SATs

Contents

Speaking and listening

Reading

Writing

National Test practice

Talking and reading aloud

What is speaking and listening?

Part of your English **Programme of Study** at school is **speaking and listening**. This is to help you to organise your thoughts to make speeches, to speak effectively to an audience, to listen to ideas and to be persuasive. It seems silly when you think about it – you learnt to speak and listen when you were a toddler, so why do you need to be taught to do it all over again?

The way you explain things, however, affects the way that people understand you, so it is worth spending some time thinking about **how to present your ideas** and thoughts in the best possible way. Well presented ideas are taken more seriously!

Top Tip

Remember – do not fidget. If you twiddle your hair or pull at your collar, people will know you are nervous – and you will feel even worse!

I LOVE reading out loud to the class.

You just love the sound of your own voice!

Reading aloud with confidence

There are some easy tips you can follow to make reading aloud less of an ordeal!

- Imagine that you are reading to a younger brother or sister rather than the whole class. Try to forget about your audience.

- Read slowly and calmly, and take deep breaths to calm yourself. When you are nervous, it is easy to rush and then you are more likely to make mistakes.

- Take notice of full stops and commas – they give you a chance to pause and take a breath.

- Practise at home in front of your family – or even in front of the mirror!

- If your throat feels tight and your mouth feels dry because you are nervous, pretend to yourself that your tongue has become incredibly heavy (without making daft faces!). This will relax you before you start to read.

Have a go...

Listen to people on the television reading the news. Think about it – they are staying calm in front of MILLIONS of people! Write some news about your week, and make a video or tape of you reading it!

Key words

speaking and listening

Quick Test

1. Why is speaking and listening part of the school curriculum?

2. Why is it important to think about how you present your ideas?

3. How can you make yourself relax as you prepare to read aloud?

4. Write and present a short presentation about a pet or hobby and read the speech to family and friends.

5. Practise reading aloud from the newspaper to your family and ask them for feedback.

Debating

Listening and presenting

You may have been told lots of times by your teachers and parents that arguing is a bad thing. Well, English is great because you are expected to be able to argue – but not about who is the most gorgeous soap star or who should be number one in the charts!

In English lessons, you will be expected to develop **debating skills**. That means listening to the views of other people and presenting your own arguments. Sometimes you will be given a topic – often a question – to think about. It could be:

- Should fox-hunting have been banned?
- Should mobile phones be allowed in class?
- Should we all be vegetarian?
- Should school uniforms be abolished?

You should think about how you feel about the issue and then compare your ideas with friends. Sharing views makes it easier to come up with good arguments. Making notes will help you to organise your ideas.

Being a good listener

When you listen to the opposing team's ideas, you should be quiet and sensible. A debate is not a free-for-all shouting match! You should **make quick notes** of things people say that you disagree with – you might want to respond to their ideas in your own speech. It is hard to do this at first, but like everything, it gets easier with practice.

Make sure you are clear about which are the **main points of their argument**. You must reply to these, so that the audience that is listening decides you have the stronger argument.

Presenting your own ideas

Discuss your **viewpoint** with your team. Sharing ideas is the best way to get organised! Try to think about the things the other team will say, so that you can have your answers ready.

If you are given time, **do some research** on your argument and find quotations from important people to back up your ideas – perhaps someone has written a report or a book on your topic. Look in the library and on the Internet.

Make notes, then re-read them and pick out the most important points. Practise remembering what these are – perhaps **make up a mnemonic** (a silly sentence using the first letter of each word you want to remember) to help you.

Top Tip

Be ready – teachers can sometimes be sneaky and ask you to prepare a speech in favour of something you do not like, such as school dinners or uniform. Alternatively, they may ask you to argue against something you love, like watching TV. They are not being mean – they are just helping you to think about the issues carefully, so you become a great speaker!

Perhaps I can talk Mum into giving me more pocket money!

Think about it carefully first or she might talk you into taking less!

Have a go...

Does your school, youth club or local Teachers' Centre have a debating team? If you enjoy presenting arguments and trying to persuade people to come round to your way of thinking, debates can be great fun!

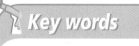

Key words

debating   mnemonic

viewpoint

Quick Test

Make notes for a speech in favour of longer lunch breaks at school. Remember to think about any arguments people may have against you, so you have a reply ready. Then present your ideas to an audience – your family, or even your class at school!

Test your skills

Carrying out research

What does a researcher do?

Lots of people do research every day, at school and at work. It means **finding out more about something**. If you were doing a history project about Vikings, you would look in the library and on the Internet for information. Researchers do the same thing to find information on the topics they are working on.

If you were a magazine researcher, one of your jobs would be to find out about topics for articles. You would look in books and on the Internet, but you would also look in newspapers and magazines. You could also find out about people's views by doing interviews. This means asking people questions.

Be a researcher

Imagine you are a researcher for a magazine for teenagers. The magazine includes articles on music, fashion, TV/film and extreme sports like parascending. You are going to do some research for an article. Choose from:

- Shark attack!

- Going vegetarian – how to break it to your parents!

- Have you got what it takes to be a pop star?

- Snowboarding – fad or sport?

Sources of information

Use the following sources of information to research the article you want to write:

- Books
- Magazines
- Newsletters
- Newsgroups on the Internet
- Information from special groups such as a sports club or conservation group

- Interviews with friends and family
- Television programmes
- Videos
- Radio programmes and interviews

Organise your ideas and then write the article. Make sure it has a beginning, middle and an end. It seems obvious, but many articles just peter out and never come to a **conclusion**.

Top Tip

*Use **quotations** from people you have interviewed, or facts you have read, to make your article lively and interesting. Do not forget to use quotation marks, and say who said what!*

> I'm going to find out about being a pop star – I think I've got what it takes!

> Only if all you need is a bad voice and dirty clothes!

Have a go...

Carry out some research on your favourite hobby, a favourite animal or a place you would like to visit. Publish your research as a report on the computer. You may even like to make a simple web page using the free sites available!

Quick Test

Without looking, name 5 good possible sources of information for carrying out research.

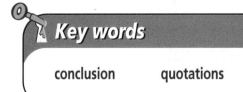

Key words

conclusion   quotations

Test your knowledge

Section 1

You are going to plan a debate in favour of wearing school uniform – which could be hard, if you do not like wearing it!

Make notes of all your ideas about wearing school uniform – both for and against. Making a spidergram of these two sets of ideas might help.

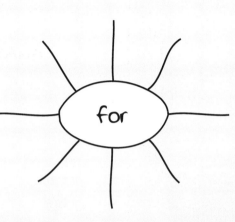

Think about these questions to help to spark your ideas.

- Is uniform more or less expensive than ordinary clothes?
- Does uniform help to make people look the same – and is that a good thing?
- What do kids wear at home?
- Is uniform smart? Is being smart important?

Section 2

Organise your ideas into arguments for and against school uniform. Arranging the information in a 'for' and 'against' table may be useful.

Do not forget to do some research for your debate. You may find articles in old newspapers or magazines to support you. Back issues (old copies) of papers and magazines can be found in the public library. You could also look on the Internet.

FOR	AGAINST

Section 3

Present your argument to an audience. You could do this at home – ask your parents to argue against school uniform, especially if they believe you should wear it! You could also ask your teacher if you could present your arguments to the class.

Top Tip *Watch people on the news or on current affairs programmes – you can often see debates and arguments.*

Reading

Reading for pleasure

We read things every day – signs, cereal packets, labels, text messages, magazines, comics, newspapers, books, emails, websites, game instructions, captions on cartoons – it is all reading! What about reading for pleasure, though?

Do you only read books at school, because your teacher tells you to? Then you do not know what you are missing! Do you ever go to the library? It's not just a place to find books for school work. You can find a whole world of exciting stories – and it's all free!

How do you decide which book to read, though?

The blurb

Do you make a habit of reading **blurbs**? A blurb is the writing on the back of a book that tells you briefly what is inside. It tells you about the **main characters and the situations** that they find themselves in. It whets your appetite for the story, leaving you hanging, so that you want to read more – which is the whole point of a blurb!

The pictures on the cover of a book can also affect whether you want to read it. Publishers spend huge amounts of money on artwork for the covers of books for that very reason. Sometimes illustrations help too.

Do you choose books because they are of a particular **genre**? That means a **particular category of books** such as adventures, thrillers, horror, romance, etc. What genre is your favourite?

Top Tip

Make sure you read a wide variety of books, both fiction and non-fiction. The more you read, the better your own writing will be.

Book reviews

Have you ever written a book review at school? Which book did you review? Why did you choose it? Book reviews can be deadly boring if you are just doing them because you have to, so why not write a review as though you were a journalist, writing for a magazine or website? Reviewers write about books, films and plays, to tell other people about them, so they can decide what to read and watch.

Pick a book that you have really enjoyed. If you love a story, you will be able to persuade other people that they should read it, because your enthusiasm will show in the words you choose.

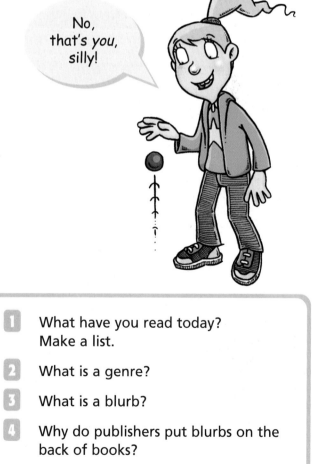

I thought a blurb was a monster from outer space!

No, that's *you*, silly!

Have a go...

Look at these great websites about books to help you to decide what to read: (http://www.myhomelibrary.org/ evenolderreaders.html) and (http://www.bbc.co.uk/cbbc/bluepeter/ bookclub/).

Key words

blurbs   genre

Quick Test

1. What have you read today? Make a list.

2. What is a genre?

3. What is a blurb?

4. Why do publishers put blurbs on the back of books?

5. What might encourage a reader to buy a book?

Reading between the lines

Looking for hidden meanings

Have you ever heard someone say that they have found something out by **reading between the lines**? It means that they have looked **behind the obvious meaning** of the words to find the **true meaning**.

When you read a book, you should read between the lines to see if there is a hidden meaning. Sometimes authors try to give us **messages** about important things, but the messages are hidden away in the stories.

Have you ever read any stories by Anne Fine? She writes excellent stories, mostly about teenagers. She wrote a book called *Flour Babies* that seems to be about a school science project, but, reading between the lines, it is really about fatherhood and how responsibilities change people.

Important messages

Authors sometimes write books by starting with the message they want to give and weaving a story around it. Sometimes though, the hidden message develops along with the story as it is written.

Dinosaurs and all that rubbish by Michael Foreman seems, at first look, to be a funny book about dinosaurs, but if you read between the lines the message is about saving the world from pollution.

Other books carry messages warning us against things. *Journey to Jo'burg* by Beverley Naidoo seems to be about a family, but it carries a message about how racism is wrong and people should not be judged according to the colour of their skin.

Top Tip

*When you are writing a **book review**, write about any 'message' you think the book contains. Refer back to the parts of the story that give you the message and this will help you to get the highest marks possible.*

Hidden meanings

Stories with hidden meanings and messages:

- *Piggybook* by Anthony Browne
- *Goggle-eyes* by Anne Fine
- *Freaky Friday* by Mary Rodgers
- *His Dark Materials* by Philip Pullman
- *The Iron Woman* by Ted Hughes
- *Wolf* by Gillian Cross
- *My Mate Shofiq* by Jan Needle

Read the books and see if you can find the true meanings by reading between the lines!

> I've just read The Lion and the Witch in the Wardrobe. It was great!

> Wasn't it rather dark, trying to read in a wardrobe?

Have a go...

See if you can find a collection of different books, all linked by a message – perhaps about the environment, relationships, honesty – whatever you like! Make a display about them, and write reviews for friends that tell them about the message.

Key words

book review

Quick Test

1. What does reading between the lines mean?

2. Can you think of a book with a message or hidden meaning?

What makes a 'good read'?

What is a good book?

When you finish a storybook, people often ask you, "Was it good?" The question is, how do you know?

Of course, whether a book is good or not can mean many things to many different people. If you enjoy a book, then you probably think it is good. Your **opinion** is also affected, however, by whether the book was about something you find interesting. Someone else might read the book, because you said it was exciting, and be disappointed, because it was not about a subject that they find interesting.

> The time travel story sounds great! I could make myself ten years older so you couldn't boss me around!

> I like the idea of ghost stories better - they might give me ideas on how to scare you!

Novels

Whatever subject a novel is about, there are certain ingredients that make it more interesting to read.

- A good strong story line
- An exciting beginning
- A strong – or surprising – ending
- Believable, realistic characters

With a good book, when you finish reading it, you feel as though you want to know more. The characters become so real to you that you want to know more about their lives and adventures. If you are really lucky, the author writes a **sequel** or even a series! Have you ever enjoyed a story so much that you were desperate to read the sequel?

Top Tip

If you like books by a particular author, do an Internet search to find out more about the author and the books they write. Keep a log book of things you want to borrow from the library – or ask for as presents!

Recommended reads

When you read a book, make a few notes to remind yourself how you felt after reading it. Keep them in a notebook – you can decorate it with stickers of pictures of book covers cut from old catalogues.

Here are some good reads to look out for:

Other Worlds

His Dark Materials – a **trilogy** of fabulous books by Philip Pullman

The Narnia Chronicles – a **series** full of fantastic characters by C.S. Lewis

The Weirdstone of Brisingamen – a book by Alan Garner that has the reader breathless with suspense!

Adventure stories

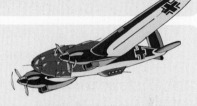

I am David by Anne Holm – a boy on an epic journey across Europe to find his family

The Machine Gunners by Robert Westall – a boy who finds a crashed Heinkel war plane during the Second World War – complete with machine gun

A Handful of Time by Kit Pearson – an excellent story about time travel

Animals

I, Houdini by Lynne Reid Banks – hilarious stories of a 'self-educated hamster'

The Black Stallion by Walter Farley – the adventures of a boy and his horse

Island of the Blue Dolphins by Scott O'Dell – the adventures of a girl alone on an island and the animals she encounters

Have a go...

Start a book group with friends, where you talk about books you have read. Ask your friends and family to recommend books to you. After reading them, talk about the story and compare ideas. You may be amazed at how different your views are!

Key words

opinion   trilogy

sequel

Quick Test

1. What makes a book a good read?

2. What 'ingredients' go into making an interesting novel?

Fiction and non-fiction

What is fiction?

Fiction is writing that comes from the author's imagination. 'Made-up' stories are fiction.

There are certain features that fiction books share:

- Fast, flowing text that you read quickly to find out what will happen next in the story.

- You read it from the beginning to the end – rather than dipping in and out – or you lose the sense of the story.

- The author's style can be very personal – as though they are talking straight to you, the reader.

- Fiction for older readers is not usually illustrated as the author relies on the words to weave a picture.

- You can often work out the meaning of new, unfamiliar words from the setting and what happens before or after in the story.

I like reading non-fiction, like books about explorers and soldiers.

I like reading fiction – so I enjoyed what you wrote in your diary about how brave you are!

What is non-fiction?

Non-fiction writing is **information**, not made-up stories. Books that tell us about history, science, the natural world and other countries are mostly non-fiction. They contain lots of true **facts**. These are the sort of books you use when you are doing a project at school.

This book is non-fiction, for example.

There are certain features that non-fiction books share:

- People often dip into non-fiction for information, rather than reading it from cover to cover.

- There are usually illustrations – including tables, diagrams and photographs – to accompany the words and to help to explain things.

- Specialised vocabulary – special words used only for particular subjects – often appears, so non-fiction books often have a **glossary**.

- The author's style is often impersonal – reporting and describing things.

- People often read non-fiction quickly, skimming through to find information they need and then re-reading the relevant sections carefully.

 Top Tip *Try to remember the differences between fiction and non-fiction – you will be expected to know them for your SATs. But remember that sometimes it is hard to tell, because people often write fiction based on real facts and events.*

Have a go...

Keep a log of books you use and read through the week. Which do you read most: fiction or non-fiction?

Key words

fiction	facts
non-fiction	glossary

Quick Test

1. Name three common features of fiction.

2. Name three common features of non-fiction.

3. What is a glossary?

4. What is skimming?

5. Are you more likely to read a fiction or non-fiction book all the way through, and why?

Authors and narrators

Who is the author?

The **author** of a piece **is the person who wrote it**. Sometimes, they write with their own **voice** – that means that they are writing about their own feelings and experiences. If you were writing your **autobiography** – the story of your life – it would all be written in your voice, because it happened to you.

On a Saturday morning, when I was a child, my dad would take my sister and me to the open market along Sydney Street. The smells, colours and sounds stay with me to this day! I would buy a huge bag of sherbet-filled chews from the market and then dive into David's Books in search of the comic books I craved, *Tales of the Unexplained*, *Astounding Stories* – I loved them all!

This passage is written in the **author's own voice**, because she is **writing about herself**.

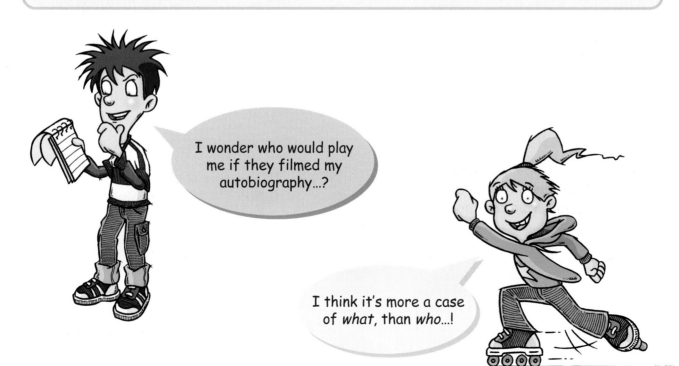

I wonder who would play me if they filmed my autobiography...?

I think it's more a case of *what*, than *who*...!

Who is the narrator?

The **narrator** is **the storyteller**. The narrator **may be the author, but is often a character** within the story. The narrator does not usually speak with the author's voice, but with his or her own voice. The narrator tells the story from his or her point of view.

Read the passage below.

I started my life lonely and unwanted. I hunted for food on rubbish tips and in bins. When it was cold, I froze. When it was wet, the rain pounded on my back. One day, I smelt a mouth-watering meaty smell. I ran to the food, cramming it into my mouth. I heard a clang and realised I was trapped in a cage!

After a terrible journey, I found myself in the darkness of a strange-smelling place. I heard a noise and one of The Hated Ones came. I hid, but she brought food and said soft words to me.

The passage above is written from the point of view of a feral cat, taken in by a family. Obviously, the cat could not be the author – they would find it hard to hold a pen! – but the cat's character is still the narrator of the passage.

Top Tip

Make sure you can use words like narrator and author when you are writing – it will help you to sound knowledgeable, and you will get higher marks for using 'book language'!

Have a go...

Next time you read a book, think about whose voice is telling the story – the author, or a narrator?

Key words

author	autobiography
voice	narrator

Quick Test

1. What does an author do?
2. What is a narrator?
3. What is the difference between an author and a narrator?
4. What is an autobiography?
5. Can a narrator ever be the same person as the author of a piece of writing?

Description and imagery

Imagery

Imagery is about making images or pictures in your mind's eye. It makes pieces of work more exciting because of the vivid descriptions. You will come across three main types of imagery:

Similes   **Metaphors**   **Personification**

Similes

Similes describe things by saying they are **like something else**.

The cat was as fluffy as a dandelion clock.

The old man's face was as wrinkly as elephant skin.

The moth danced around the lamp like a prima ballerina.

The monkey scratched her head, looking like a puzzled child.

Top Tip

Look for the words 'like' or 'as' in a description to help you to spot a simile – you can see them in the examples above.

I'd say I was as strong as metal!

Well, I'd say you smell as strong as rotten fish!

Metaphors

Metaphors describe things by saying **they *are* something else**.

The slug was a rubber tube, lying on the path.

The newt was a tiny dragon, lurking behind a rock.

The baby was a siren, sounding in the night.

The blackberry was a jewel, shining in the sunlight.

Personification

Personification describes things by giving human **characteristics to non-human things**.

The tree was a tall dancer, her green skirt swirling in the breeze.

Winter is a wicked old man, pinching children's cheeks with his cold fingers.

My tiredness cuddled me to sleep, like my mother's arms.

The shadows followed me, like an assassin in a dark cloak.

Have a go...

When you are reading – books, magazines, advertisements – look for imagery. Make a note of any really good examples in a writing notebook and use them to help you to make your own work more exciting.

Key words

imagery	personification
similes	characteristics
metaphors	

Quick Test

1. What is a simile? Give an example.

2. What is a metaphor? Give an example.

3. What is personification? Give an example.

Onomatopoeia and alliteration

Special effects

Sometimes poets and authors use **special effects** when they are writing, **to set a mood or create an image**.

Onomatopoeia means words that sound like the things they describe:

Smash   Bang   Clang   Pop   Fizz   Crunch   Flash

Alliteration

Alliteration is where the consonant sounds in words are repeated:

Beautiful Bethany baked bagels, buns and bread for breakfast.

The 'b' sound is repeated and the sentence is full of alliteration (as well as baked goods!).

Tongue-twisters often use alliteration and that is why they are so tricky! Try:

Biting big baked buns, Betty burped boldly!

Assonance is when vowel sounds are repeated:

Try to light the fire, Maia!

Top Tip

Make sure you can use words like alliteration and onomatopoeia when you are asked to talk about poems – it will win you extra marks.

Silly Sam sucks at sums – Oh, I do love alliteration!

Sam rhymes with 'bam!' and 'wham!' – and they're both onomatapoeic!

Have a go...

Write a tongue-twister that is full of alliteration – and teach it to your friends!

Key words

onomatopoeia   assonance
alliteration

Quick Test

1. Which of these words are onomatopoeic?

   baby   drip   squash   splash
   bottle   pop

2. Which words would fill the gaps to make these sentences alliterate?

   Saucy Susie   drank sipped gargled   soda slowly.

   Greedy Grant   grabbed took pinched   Gordon's grapes.

   Tabitha tasted   nine ten eleven   tiny treats.

3. What is alliteration?

4. What is assonance?

Ambiguity

What is ambiguity?

Ambiguity is a difficult word – but when teachers are marking work, they find lots of it! Ambiguity means that **the meaning of a sentence is unclear**. Read this sentence:

The girl put the cat out, because she was noisy.

What does it mean? Did the girl put the cat out, because the cat was noisy, or did the girl put the cat out, because the girl was noisy? The meaning of the sentence is unclear, so it is an ambiguous sentence.

How about, "The dog sniffed the bin, because it was smelly."? That's ambiguous!

The only smelly thing around here is you – and that's certain!

Spot the real meaning!

Read these sentences – what do you think the writer meant in each case?

The dog chased the cat, because it was bored.

The cat or the dog – which was bored? Was the dog trying to cheer the cat up, because the cat was bored, or was the dog looking for mischief because the dog was bored?

The teacher scolded the girl, because she was being nasty.

The teacher or the girl – who was nasty? Was the teacher telling the girl off, because she was a horrible, grumpy teacher, or did the girl get scolded because she was being naughty?

The mother cuddled her baby, because she was crying.

Who was crying – the mother or the baby?

It is important to make your meaning clear! Imagine if you said, "If that cat doesn't want her food, throw it away," and your Mum threw the cat in the bin...!

Top Tip *Always read your work back to yourself when you have finished, to check that your meanings are clear. What seems clear when you write it does not always seem so clear when you read it. The examiners will see fewer howlers – and you will get higher marks!*

Have a go...

Sometimes meaning becomes unclear, because the sentence you are writing goes on and on and on and on ... It is better sometimes to use shorter sentences to make your meanings clear.

Key words

ambiguity

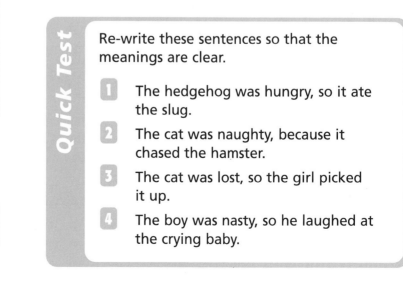

Quick Test

Re-write these sentences so that the meanings are clear.

1. The hedgehog was hungry, so it ate the slug.
2. The cat was naughty, because it chased the hamster.
3. The cat was lost, so the girl picked it up.
4. The boy was nasty, so he laughed at the crying baby.

Special words

Special words

English has a **special vocabulary all of its own** – words that you need to learn, so you can talk about them. The words on this page are to do with reading. You will already know that an author is a person who writes books and an illustrator is a person who draws the pictures. You will also know that books have a title – what they are called. But did you know that a book has an **ISBN**? It stands for International Standard Book Number and is used by bookshops and libraries.

Footnotes and parenthesis

These are special words that give the reader extra information about what they are reading.

Footnotes are found at the foot, or bottom, of the page. Footnotes are used **to explain hard words** in a piece of writing. Sometimes they are used to give the reader extra information.

Parenthesis means words that are added in brackets to a piece of writing to give us more information.

Sometimes words in parenthesis are explanations:

- The boy (who had already been to the shop) said he would go to buy the milk.

Sometimes words in parenthesis are afterthoughts:

- I will be on the football team this year! (I hope…)

More special words

Appendix

An appendix is a collection of extra information added at the end of a book. If a book was about insects, the appendix could have information about which flowers to plant to attract butterflies.

Glossary

A glossary is a collection of words. You find them in non-fiction books. There is a glossary in this book. All the words that are difficult to understand are in red, to show that they are in the glossary. The meanings of the words are given, so you can learn new words.

Index

The index is a list of words, found at the back of a book, which tells you which page contains the things you are looking for. They are arranged in alphabetical order to make finding things easier.

Top Tip

Make sure you can use the special words described on these pages – and that you use the things described in your own work. This will help your work to be more polished, and you will get higher marks.

I don't think the word 'annoying' is listed!

Have a go...

Look at some non-fiction books at the library. Can you identify and use the glossary, index and footnotes?

Do you think I'll be mentioned in the glossary of this book?

Key words

ISBN	appendix
footnotes	glossary
parenthesis	index

Quick Test

1. What is an ISBN?
2. What is a footnote?
3. What is an appendix?
4. What does parenthesis mean?
5. What is a glossary for?

Life stories

Special types of writing

You may have heard these words before:

- **Curriculum Vitae (CV)**
- **Biography**
- **Autobiography**

All these special types of text tell us about people's lives.

A Curriculum Vitae is a record of what exams people have passed, what other qualifications they have and what jobs they have done. People use them when they are applying for jobs.

Read this CV:

Name:	Sheila Huggins
Education:	School Leaving Certificate
Work:	Hassans Jewellers until birth of son, Stephen, in 1953
	Own business as jeweller 1970 – 1983
	Agar's Jewellers 1983 – retirement in 1999

Biographies

A biography is the story of someone's life.

Sheila Huggins left school as soon as she was allowed to – not because she wanted to, but because she had to earn a living. She was lucky and was taken on as an apprentice at Hassans, a renowned jewellery workshop, where she learnt her trade. She worked, like so many other women at the time, until she had her son, Stephen. Sheila used her talents to earn money at home, running her own business until 1983, when her youngest daughter started senior school. Sheila carried out many amazing pieces of work, including repairs to a Witch Doctor's neckpiece – reputed to curse her if she did a bad job! – and the famous pearl and sapphire necklace worn by Diana, Princess of Wales, in her engagement photographs.

Suggested activities

What activities can your club do?

- Review books.

- Make up plays using stories you have read.

- Keep reading journals and diaries.

- Write and make books for younger children.

- Keep a scrapbook of book reviews found in newspapers and magazines.

- Make your own reading club web page where other people can read your reviews.

- Hotseat – just like in drama, imagine you are a particular character from a book and answer questions (as the character would answer).

- Write letters to your favourite authors. You can often find contact details on publisher websites.

- Make sure you look at different genres (horror, adventure, mystery, fantasy) – you may find a whole new set of books to read that you had never considered!

- Send reviews to websites such as ACHUKA (www.achuka.co.uk/).

Top Tip

Look for book review sites for children on the Internet, such as Wordpool (www.wordpool.co.uk) – and see if other people can recommend any great new books for your club to read.

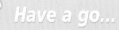

Have a go...

Make a group reading journal in a scrapbook or folder. Cut pictures of book covers from old book catalogues (ask at your local book shop or library) or print them off from publisher websites. Keep your cover clean by covering it in clear sticky plastic. Show your teacher!

Test your knowledge

Comprehension test

Read the passages, then answer the questions.

Remember:

- Skim-read the text
- Read the questions and find the key words
- Scan the text for the answers.

Section 1

The Legend of Zelda – The Ocarina of Time

This game is full of exciting and imaginative characters and adventures. Link, the hero, tries to stop Ganondorf, the evil wizard, from collecting three magical gems: the Kokiri Emerald, the Goron Ruby and the Zora Sapphire. These jewels, along with the Ocarina of Time and the Sacred Sword, allow the holder to enter the Sacred Realm.

Ganondorf wants to enter the Sacred Realm to take control of the Tri force, the source of ultimate power. The Tri force is made up of three elements: Power, Wisdom and Bravery. If someone evil tries to take control of the Tri force, it will split into three parts. Ganondorf will take Power and will be able to corrupt the world.

1   What is the hero of The Legend of Zelda called?

2   Who is Ganondorf?

3   Why does Ganondorf want to enter the Sacred Realm?

4   What is the Tri force made up from?

5   What happens if an evil person takes control of the Tri force?

So Ring-a-roses is about the plague?

Section 2

The Black Death

The Black Death, a terrible plague, reached England in 1348. It spread from the port of Weymouth to Bristol and, in spite of closing the roads, quickly spread to Gloucester. It then passed to Oxford and from there to London. By the spring it was at its height. It seemed to attack men rather than women, and the young and strong rather than the elderly.

The plague continued to ravage Europe for centuries. The Tudor period saw repeated plagues. People carried sponges soaked in vinegar and posies of flowers, called tussie-mussies, to ward off the plague fumes. They did not realise that the plague was carried by the fleas on the rats they saw everywhere.

The nursery rhyme 'Ring-a-ring o' roses' dates from the time of the plague:

- *Ring-a-ring o' roses,* (The rash, that came with the plague, appeared in red rings on the skin.)

- *A pocket full of posies,* (The tussie-mussies that people carried to ward off the plague.)

- *Ah-tishoo! Ah-tishoo!* (Sneezing – a symptom of the plague.)

- *We all fall down.* (Everyone dies.)

1   When did the plague reach England?

2   Who seemed most likely to be infected by the plague?

3   How did people try to avoid the plague?

4   What was the plague really caused by?

5   What do the lines 'Ah-tishoo! Ah-tishoo! We all fall down' refer to?

Top Tip

Remember to read the passages right through carefully before you read the questions – and then read them again, scanning for key words. That way you will pick up maximum marks.

Yuck! And I thought it was just a sweet, little kids' rhyme!

Clauses

What is a clause?

A **clause** is a part of a sentence. It has a subject and a verb. It is not a sentence, so it does not have to start with a capital letter or end with a full stop.

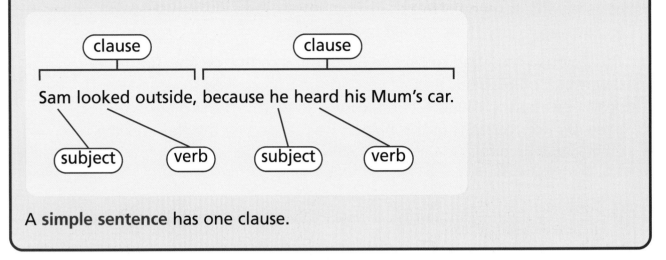

A **simple sentence** has one clause.

Compound sentences

Compound sentences have **two important clauses**. Each clause would make a simple sentence on its own, but are joined to make a compound sentence. Words such as 'and', 'because' and 'so' are used to join the clauses to make a compound sentence.

> She jumped in the air. She was excited.
>
> She jumped in the air, because she was excited.

Each clause **makes sense on its own** and each clause is as important as the other.

Complex sentences

A **complex sentence** is **built around a main clause and also has less important clauses**. The main clause is the most important part of the sentence and contains the main idea. It would make sense on its own.

The less important clauses are called **subordinate clauses**.

(main clause)   (subordinate clause)

Helen ran quickly, because she saw the ice-cream van.

HAPPY'S ICE-CREAM

Top Tip *Remember, a clause has a subject and a verb – or it is not a clause!*

I'm really complex – does that make me important?

No – you're just a subordinate!

Have a go...

Read a magazine article, and underline the different types of sentence (simple, complex and compound) in different colours.

Key words

clause

simple sentence

compound sentence

complex sentence

main clause

subordinate clause

Quick Test

1 What is a simple sentence? Give an example.

2 What is a clause?

3 What is a complex sentence? Give an example.

4 What is a compound sentence? Give an example.

Contractions

What are contractions?

Contractions are **words that have letters missing**. An **apostrophe** shows where the letters have been missed out. Words like this are used in informal writing, such as:

- Letters to friends

- When a character in a story is speaking

- Contractions are not used in pieces of **formal writing**, such as reports, formal letters and certificates.

Top Tip

Remember, do not use contractions in formal writing – it could lose you marks in a test, for example, if you were writing a formal letter.

Contractions

These are examples of contractions:

I cannot → I can't
I am → I'm
I have → I've
we are → we're
does not → doesn't
I had → I'd
I would → I'd
they are → they're
he will → he'll
she will → she'll
who is → who's
shall not → shan't
will not → won't
you have → you've
you are → you're

she is → she's
he is → he's
did not → didn't
is not → isn't
should not → shouldn't

won't!

Have a go...

*Look at **dialogue** in a story (where characters are speaking). You will see that contractions are often used, because speech is often **informal**. Re-write the dialogue, changing the contractions to full words. Read it aloud. Does it sound more formal?*

Key words

contractions   dialogue
apostrophe   informal
formal writing

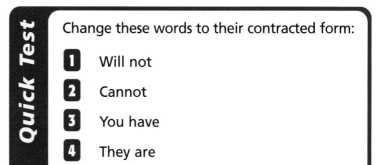

Quick Test

Change these words to their contracted form:

1 Will not

2 Cannot

3 You have

4 They are

Possessive apostrophes

To show 'belonging'

Apostrophes can be used to show that something belongs to somebody.

They are called **possessive apostrophes**.

To show something belongs to somebody, **add an apostrophe followed by an s.**

The bowl that belongs to the cat ➔ the cat's bowl

The drink that belongs to the woman ➔ the woman's drink

The book that belongs to the boy ➔ the boy's book

Possessives ending in 's'

What happens when a word already ends in 's'?

When a word already ends in 's', the apostrophe is sometimes added without adding another s.

> The sister belonging to James → James' sister

But other times, another s is added.

> The hospital established by St Thomas → St Thomas's Hospital

Top Tip

When the word ending in 's' is a group of people, an apostrophe is added without an 's'.
The gardens belonging to our neighbours → our neighbours' gardens

Sam's very possessive about his scooter!

And Mel's even more possessive about her sweets!

Have a go...

Do some Internet research and see if you can find out what is meant by a 'greengrocer's apostrophe'. Have you seen any examples when you are out and about in town?

Key words

possessive apostrophes

Quick Test

Add the possessive apostrophes to these sentences:

1. The cats fur was matted.
2. The girls eyes were blue.
3. The dogs collar was red.
4. The boys hair was blond.
5. St. Jamess Church Fair is on Saturday.

Punctuation

Making sense

Punctuation helps to make writing make sense. Without punctuation, passages would just be a collection of words.

Read this passage:

> The dog ran around the garden chasing hens it was brown and the hens were white yesterday the dog dug up lots of flowers in the flowerbed.

It does not make much sense, does it?

Read it again, with the punctuation:

> The dog ran around the garden, chasing hens. It was brown and the hens were white. Yesterday, the dog dug up lots of flowers in the flowerbed.

It makes more sense with punctuation!

Top Tip *Always read your work back to yourself to make sure you have used the correct punctuation and that your work makes sense.*

Ending sentences

Full stops are put at the end of a sentence to show it has finished. Question marks go at the end of a sentence when it is a question. Exclamation marks are used at the end of a sentence showing surprise or fear – an exclamation, in other words. Exclamations are used to show someone is shouting. You use a question mark or an exclamation mark instead of a full stop. When you start a new sentence, you use a capital letter.

Is that my coat?

That's my coat!

Commas

Commas are used to divide different parts of a sentence. Commas help to make things clear.

Commas separate main clauses from subordinate clauses in complex sentences (see pages 38–39).

Without a comma:

> When the play was over the people went home.

With a comma:

> When the play was over, the people went home.

The meaning is made clear with the use of a comma. In the first sentence, it could sound as though the play was over the people!

I LIKE EXCLAMATION MARKS, BECAUSE I LIKE SHOUTING!

You would!

Have a go...

Re-write a passage from a book you are reading without punctuation. Does it make sense or does it mean something different? Are any of the meanings ambiguous without the punctuation?

Quick Test

1 Why is correct punctuation important?

2 What are commas used for?

3 When are exclamation marks used?

4 Which of these sentences should end with a question mark?

   a He asked me why I had read that book

   b Why did you read that book

Key words

punctuation

Writing speech

Reported speech

Reported speech means someone is telling the reader about **something somebody else has said.**

Then he said he was going home.

The man shouted hello as he came into the room.

The teacher told us all to put our hands up.

Reported speech does not use **speech marks**.

This does not mean you can just repeat exactly the words a person says.

For example: If your mum said, "Don't be rude to my sister," you might report it as: Mum told us not to upset Auntie.

Speech marks

Speech marks are used when **someone is actually speaking**.

"I'm going home!" said the man.

When somebody starts to speak, **the words inside speech marks always start with a capital letter**, even if they are not at the beginning of a sentence.

Then the girl said, "I like cats, even if they have fleas!"

Speech marks always end with a punctuation mark inside the speech marks. If someone is surprised or shouting, use an exclamation mark. If it is a question, use a question mark.

Remember – speech marks are only used when someone is actually speaking.

Have a go...

Make a list of all the different words you can use instead of said, e.g. 'asked', 'laughed', 'exclaimed'... It will make your work much more interesting! Make a poster on the computer with the title 'Not just SAID but...' and add the different words in lots of fonts and colours.

Key words

reported speech

speech marks

Quick Test

Add speech marks where necessary to these sentences:

1 The boy said that he hated mashed potato.

2 I like science fiction films best, said Melanie.

3 Would you like a sweet? asked Bethany.

4 The woman told me that she was a doctor.

5 I hate cold weather, said Eleanor, but I love the snow!

Plurals

Adding 's'

When you are **writing or talking about more than one thing, it is called a plural.**
Usually, you just write a word and add an 's' to the end to make it a plural:

cat ➔ cats   bird ➔ birds

flower ➔ flowers   chair ➔ chairs

But there are some words that are a bit trickier!

If a word already ends in 's', you cannot add
another 's'! Instead, you add es.

dress ➔ dresses   mess ➔ messes   press ➔ presses

Words ending in 'y'

Words that end in 'y' have special rules – but it is still confusing!

Most words that end in 'y' lose the 'y' and add ies:

lady ➔ ladies   pony ➔ ponies

baby ➔ babies   puppy ➔ puppies

But there are some exceptions

donkey ➔ donkeys

just to confuse you!

So would the plural of Sam be Sams?

Yuk, I can't cope with you being anything other than singular!

Words ending in 'f'

When words ending in 'f' change from single to plural, **the 'f' almost always changes to ves**.

leaf ➔ leaves

hoof ➔ hooves

calf ➔ calves

dwarf ➔ dwarves

Words ending in 'o'

When words ending in 'o' change from single to plural, there is a special rule: 'o' adds es

tomato ➔ tomatoes   potato ➔ potatoes

But – you guessed – there are exceptions!

piano ➔ pianos

Top Tip

Some words have strange plurals – and you just have to learn them! Learn these:
- *mouse ➔ mice*
- *child ➔ children*
- *goose ➔ geese.*

Can you find any more?

Have a go...

Learn tricky plurals by writing the single version of the word on one side of a piece of paper and the plural on the other side – then test yourself.

Key words

plural

Quick Test

Write the plurals of these words.

1 dog

2 piano

3 calf

4 baby

5 potato

Nouns

What do we mean by nouns?

A noun is a naming word. It may be a thing, a person or a place.

There are three types of nouns you need to know about and identify:

Common nouns   **Proper nouns**   **Collective nouns**

Common nouns

Common nouns are the general names of things.

dog   cat   cow   horse   boy   girl   man
woman   table   chair   television   computer

 *Every sentence has a noun – see if you can identify nouns in sentences as you read them.*

Proper nouns

Proper nouns are the names of particular people, places or things. They have a **capital letter**.

Bethany   Luke   Durham   Brighton

Collective nouns

Collective nouns name groups of things.

They have special names for different groups, but some of the most common include:

Army of soldiers

Herd of cows

Flock of seagulls

So, a bunch of bananas is a collective noun?

Yes, and it's a monkey's breakfast!

Have a go...

Can you think of any other collective nouns? See if you can find any in today's newspaper.

Key words

common nouns   collective nouns

proper nouns

Quick Test

Are these proper, collective or common nouns?

1 Newcastle Upon Tyne

2 cat

3 family

4 mum

5 girl

Verbs

What are verbs?

Verbs are the words that describe actions. Every sentence has to have a verb or it is not a sentence! Verbs tell you what a person or thing is doing.

The girl is jumping.

The word jumping is the verb.

eek!

The mouse squeaked.

The word squeaked is the verb.

The slug slithered.

The word slithered is the verb.

The boy is playing football.

The word playing is the verb.

Passive verbs

Passive verbs tell you about what is being done. A sentence with a **passive verb tells you about the thing or person that the action is happening to**. It does not always say what or who is doing the action, though!

The table was polished.

Active verbs

Active verbs tell you what is being done by someone or something.

> Beth rang her friends.   Lila chased the mouse.

Tenses

Verbs change **tense** to show us when things happen: past, present (now) and future.

> I ate the chocolate ice-cream – past.
>
> I am eating the chocolate ice-cream – present (now).
>
> I shall eat the chocolate ice-cream – future.

Top Tip

When you are writing, read your work through to make sure you do not jump from one tense to another and back again. Sometimes, teachers read stories that sound like they have taken place in a time machine because of all the flipping backwards and forwards!

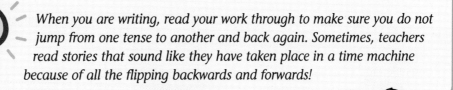

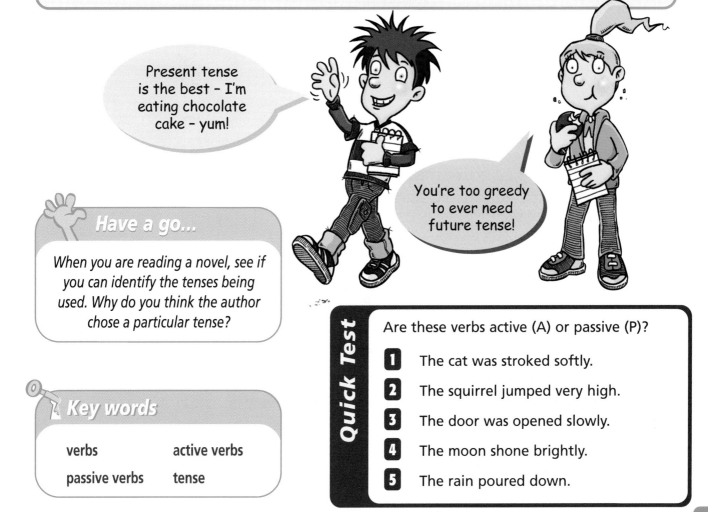

Present tense is the best – I'm eating chocolate cake – yum!

You're too greedy to ever need future tense!

Have a go...

When you are reading a novel, see if you can identify the tenses being used. Why do you think the author chose a particular tense?

Key words

verbs	active verbs
passive verbs	tense

Quick Test

Are these verbs active (A) or passive (P)?

1. The cat was stroked softly.
2. The squirrel jumped very high.
3. The door was opened slowly.
4. The moon shone brightly.
5. The rain poured down.

Adjectives

What are adjectives?

Adjectives are **describing words**. They **describe a noun** in a sentence.

The huge squid slithered into the dark cave.

'Huge' is the adjective that describes 'squid', and 'dark' is the adjective that describes 'cave'.

The stinking rubbish was rotting on the enormous tip.

'Stinking' is the adjective that describes 'rubbish', and 'enormous' is the adjective that describes 'tip'.

The glittering snow sparkled like white sugar.

'Glittering' is the adjective that describes 'snow', and 'white' is the adjective that describes 'sugar'.

Top Tip

Make a note of your favourite, most descriptive adjectives in a special notebook when you are reading, and try to use them in your own work.

Making your writing exciting

Adjectives are a **powerful tool** for a writer. They are describing words, and descriptions are what make people want to read more. Adjectives can help to make **vivid word pictures** in the mind of your reader.

Compare these sentences:

- The snail slithered across the path.
- The delicate, pink snail slithered across the mossy, tiled path.

Which sentence makes the best word picture? The sentence with adjectives, of course!

- The poppy petals blew away on the wind.
- The scarlet, silken poppy petals blew away on the warm wind.

Which sentence makes the best word picture? Once again, the sentence with adjectives.

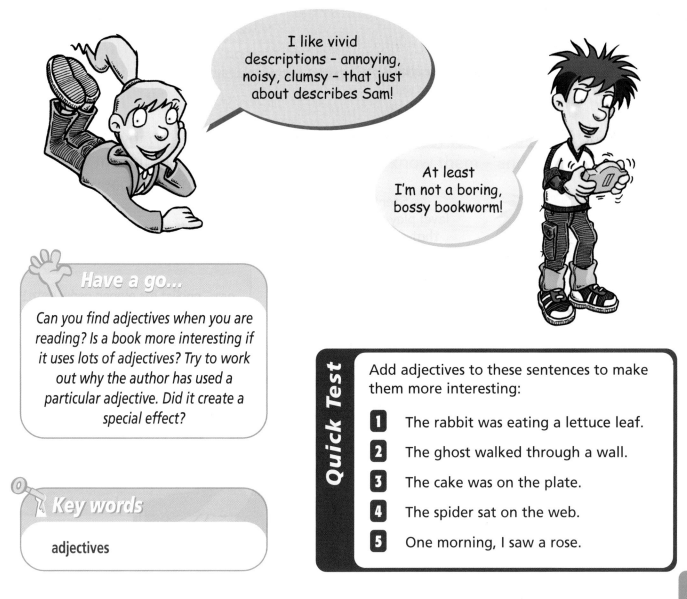

I like vivid descriptions – annoying, noisy, clumsy – that just about describes Sam!

At least I'm not a boring, bossy bookworm!

Have a go...

Can you find adjectives when you are reading? Is a book more interesting if it uses lots of adjectives? Try to work out why the author has used a particular adjective. Did it create a special effect?

Key words

adjectives

Quick Test

Add adjectives to these sentences to make them more interesting:

1. The rabbit was eating a lettuce leaf.
2. The ghost walked through a wall.
3. The cake was on the plate.
4. The spider sat on the web.
5. One morning, I saw a rose.

Writers creating moods

Using language

When you read a passage in your Year Six SATs exam (National Test), you may be asked how the author has used language to create a particular mood or feeling.

Read this passage. It was written by a boy in Year Six, who had been studying Romeo and Juliet. He is retelling the story of Scene One.

As you read, try to **think about how he has used language to create the right mood** for the piece.

The families meet in the street and animosity flares.

'Are you insulting us?' asked a Capulet of a nearby group of jeering Montagues.

'I do insult,' the young man sneered.

'But do you insult us?' a Capulet questioned.

'Raise your swords and drown the Capulets in their own blood!' bellowed a Montague.

The Capulets rushed the Montagues, swinging their swords, and the Montagues parried their blows. Blood flew from wounds inflicted by biting blades. Screams of anguish and victorious yells echoed through the surrounding alleys. Blood trickled thickly among the cobbles.

How did he do it?

The passage is very effective and the boy got a good mark for the piece of work that the passage is taken from. The passage is about the way that the two families, the Montagues and the Capulets, fight and the hatred they feel for one another.

The passage uses interesting **vocabulary** such as 'animosity', 'jeering' and 'sneered'. They sound right for the Shakespearian subject being discussed. He uses **alliteration** (see page 25) to describe the action – 'biting blades', which sounds like a sword cutting flesh.

'Screams of anguish and victorious yells' is much more interesting than using words such as 'shouting' – the writer has thought about using varied and interesting vocabulary.

'Blood trickled thickly among the cobbles' makes a vivid – but horrific – picture in the reader's mind's eye and this helps to build the idea that the play is going to be violent and bloody – which it is!

Top Tip

When you are reading a story, always think about the way the author builds the mood. If it is a suspense story, for example, the author may have used very short sentences to add tension to the story. When you are writing about a story, point out the way moods have been created, to gain better marks.

Sluggish scooter more like!

I like biting blades – nearly as cool as my sizzling scooter!

Have a go...

Read different genres of story and see if you can work out how the author sets the scene and builds atmosphere – then use the same strategies in your own stories!

Key words

vocabulary   alliteration

Quick Test

Which words or phrases in the passage on page 60 do you feel build the mood of suspense and brewing violence? Highlight them with a marker pen.

How English is English?

A mixed bag

English is a language that has developed over hundreds of years, and each time a different group has invaded the island, they have brought their words with them! British people who have travelled to other countries have also brought back words with them that have become part of the language. These are called **loanwords**.

Words from India

Hindi is a language spoken in Northern India. Lots of Hindi words have become part of the English language. They were used by many British people who lived and worked in India during the time when Britain had an **Empire** – when it controlled other countries.

'Bangle', 'cot', 'chutney', 'jodhpurs', 'loot', 'jungle' and 'thug' are all words that have come to English via **Hindi** words!

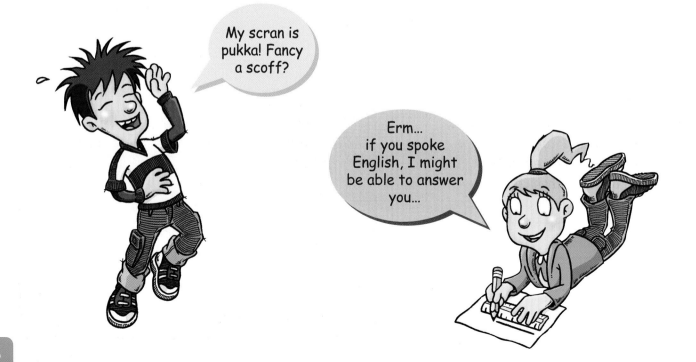

My scran is pukka! Fancy a scoff?

Erm… if you spoke English, I might be able to answer you…

Romani words

Many words in the English language come from **Romani** – the language spoken by Romany or Gypsy people.

'Posh', 'pal', and 'lollipop' all come from Romani. So do lots of **slang** words, such as 'charver'!

Dialect

Dialect means words, phrases and pronunciations that are used in a particular place.

These words are used in and around Newcastle. The dialect is often called 'geordie'.

> scran – food   chore/chaw – steal   radge – crazy, enraged

These words and phrases are used in and around London. The dialect is often called 'cockney'.

> mush – mate
>
> put the mockers on – jinx

The interesting thing is, both the Geordie words and the Cockney words derive from Romani words!

Top Tip

Language grows and changes over time, with new words being added to the official Oxford dictionary every year. Can you find out which ones were added this year?

Have a go...

Do some Internet research to find out more about where English words come from. Make a list of words, showing the countries or languages the words came from. Think of a way to store and organise your findings using ICT.

Key words

loanwords

Quick Test

Do some research in books or on the Internet to find out where these words come from:

1. shampoo
2. pukka
3. dungaree
4. algebra
5. gymkhana

Drama

Performing

Do you like **drama**? Plays can be interesting to read, but they are written to be performed. They are much more exciting to watch at the theatre, or even to act in yourself!

Acting gives you a chance to pretend to be someone else. That can be someone – or something (think of the Cybermen or Daleks in Dr Who!) – quite unlike your own character.

Be a playwright!

Get together with your friends and **devise** a play together. Make sure there is plenty of action, and chances to dress up and face paint! Use your story to carry a message or a **theme**. You can use **special dramatic techniques** such as **flashbacks** to make your play more interesting.

You can improve your own writing by **evaluating** the plays and films you watch on TV. Think about the way the writer has used language to convey his or her ideas. Then evaluate how well the actors have interpreted their roles.

Top Tip

When you are playing a part, try to imagine how the character would feel as things happen. That will help you to act 'in character'! Try 'hot seating', where you answer questions your friends ask you as your character would answer them.

Reading plays

When you read a play, you will find it looks very different to a novel. Most of the play is written in dialogue – what the characters say. That is because plays are supposed to be performed, more than read! The names of the characters appear next to the things they say, so the actors know when it is their turn to speak.

You will also see stage directions. These are instructions to tell the actors what is happening around them, and special things they should do.

I LOVE acting! I could do it all day long!

Yeah - you can trust Mel to make a drama out of ANYTHING!

Have a go...

Find a local drama group or workshop and join. You get to play some fun games, and even put on plays for an audience. If you do not want to get involved as a performer, you can get involved as a writer or technical helper.

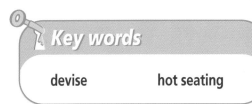

Key words

| devise | hot seating |

Quick Test

Watch a film on the TV. Write a profile of a character. How does he or she walk/talk/act? How does this tell the audience about the sort of person he or she is?

Writing instructions

Imperatives

Instructions tell you what to do. Instructions on signs, such as 'No right turn', or in recipes or craft books do not *ask* you to do something; they *tell* you. They are written using something called the **imperative**.

The imperative uses the verb (the 'doing' word) without 'to' or any other **noun** or **pronoun** in front of it. An imperative would say:

'Fold the paper'

rather than

'you need to fold the paper'.

You can see imperative instructions around you – in recipes, on signs, medicine, notices or food packaging, for example.

Chocolate bananas

You need:

3 bananas

200g chocolate

100g grated nuts

1   *Peel* the bananas.
2   *Melt* the chocolate.
3   *Dip* the bananas in the chocolate.
4   *Roll* the bananas in the nuts.
5   *Leave* the chocolate to set.

Signs give imperative instructions too.

What do they look like?

Imperative instructions are not written as sentences. They are often written as lists or bulleted points. You need to start at the beginning and work your way through **chronologically**. If you follow the instructions in the wrong order, or miss out steps, you may end up with a strange result!

Top Tip

Look at a recipe in a magazine. Can you identify the imperative instructions? Highlight them with a felt pen.

Go away, you beast!

Well, that was pretty imperative...

Have a go...

Make sure you can write instructions properly, using the imperative. Invent a new recipe for a dessert or a smoothie, and write it on a piece of card. Then follow the instructions to make a treat for your friends!

Key words

noun	chronologically
pronoun	

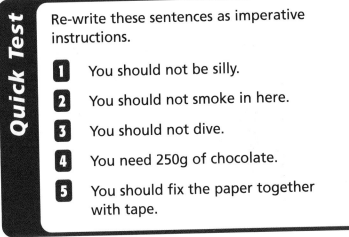

Quick Test

Re-write these sentences as imperative instructions.

1. You should not be silly.
2. You should not smoke in here.
3. You should not dive.
4. You need 250g of chocolate.
5. You should fix the paper together with tape.

67

Writing a recount

What is a recount?

Recounts tell people about something that has happened. They are written in the past tense. Recounts need to be written in **chronological order** – in the order in which something happened.

A recount could be:

An **anecdote**

An account of a visit

A retelling of the story of an event in history

A **biographical** piece of writing

Time lines

To organise your writing, make sure you have your ideas in chronological order. A good way of sketching this out quickly is to use a **time line**.

Here is a time line for a piece of **autobiographical** writing:

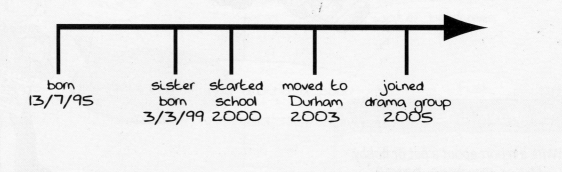

born
13/7/95

sister
born
3/3/99

started
school
2000

moved to
Durham
2003

joined
drama group
2005

To create a time line, draw a long arrow across your piece of paper. For each event, draw a line that cuts through the time line and make your note.

Drawing a flow chart

Alternatively, you could draw a **flow chart** to help you to get things in the correct order.

| born 13/7/95 | → | sister born 3/3/99 | → | started school 2000 | → | moved to Durham 2003 | → | joined drama group 2005 |

Either method gives you an opportunity to sort out in your own head the main events that you need to include in your recount, and it puts them into the correct order, or sequence.

Once you have made your plan, you can use it to write your recount. Each point in your diagram becomes a sentence or paragraph in your recount.

Top Tip

The time line is a short, sketched-out plan, so do not spend too much time on it – it is a tool to organise your ideas quickly. This is very useful in a test situation!

Have a go...

Think about what you did yesterday. Sketch out a flow chart to describe what you did, in order.

Key words

biographical

autobiographical

Quick Test

Choose a person you admire and do some research about their life. Organise your ideas by writing a time line. Do not forget to divide it into sections! Then expand the sections into sentences and paragraphs to write a biographical piece of writing about the person.

Improving your writing skills

Stages of writing

Whatever type of writing you are doing – a story, a report, a leaflet – there are stages you need to go through to make your writing as good as it possibly can be. The best writers all follow these steps – even your favourite **novelist**!

Research

Do not start to write until you have researched your topic (see page 8). Your sources of information might include books, websites and interviews.

Planning

Writers spend lots of time thinking! They prepare for their writing by considering ideas, organising their thoughts and making notes. Creating a plan helps you to get all of your ideas down on paper, so you do not need to worry about forgetting anything. This leaves you free to think about powerful words and phrases to use so you can get your ideas across effectively.

Drafting

Authors write many drafts of work before they get to the final version. A **rough draft** helps your writing to take shape without you getting distracted from the flow of your writing by worrying about spellings, paragraphs, etc. Drafting helps you to rehearse sentences and decide which words to use. Do not be afraid to cross things out at this stage and make substitutions of better, stronger words! You might reread a piece you have written and decide to add a metaphor or perhaps some alliteration, to make a powerful idea.

Revising and editing

Once you have written a first draft, read it aloud to hear how it sounds. Does it flow and make sense? Have you missed out anything important? Make alterations until you are satisfied. This is what an **editor** does when a book is being produced!

Proof reading

The final stage is to **proofread** your work. That means checking spellings and grammar, etc.

 Proofread carefully and you will not lose marks in a test situation for silly mistakes.

I'd like to be a famous novelist one day...

You, famous? That WOULD be novel!

Have a go...

Write something, such as the opening paragraph of a story, and ask a group of friends to do the same. Swap the openings and 'mark' them as though you were an editor. How could they be improved (make sure your comments are positive). You have your very own critique group, like a professional author!

 **Key words**

proofread

Quick Test

Carry out a piece of writing – on whatever subject you prefer. Go through every stage, from research to proofreading, over the course of a few days. Make sure you know how to follow all of the stages easily until it comes as 'second nature'!

Story writing process 1

Beginning a story

What makes you want to read a story? Once you have got past the cover and possibly read the **blurb** on the back, **it is the opening sentences that hook** you and make you want to read more.

Read these story starters

The girl huddled into the damp corner of the alley, pressing herself back into the darkness. Her breath came in sobs – what if they heard her?

"Come back here, boy!" boomed the angry voice. The scruffy boy scrabbled out through the doorway into the sunshine. Parcels of food crammed his bulging pockets. His family was starving and he, as the man of the family now, was not about to let that happen.

A tentacle uncoiled slowly, like a vast rubbery rope. It felt about delicately, probing rock crevices and holes for something to eat. Then it gently touched the toes of the boy, who felt a touch like a tiny crab scuttling across his feet.

Do they make you want to read more?

Top Tip

*Read, read, read – then read some more! The more stories you read, the better your own stories will become, as you learn about different **genres** and styles of writing and the way they 'work'.*

Writing your own stories

Think about the story starters you have just read. Did you like any of them? Each was written to make you wonder what happens next. In story one, what is chasing the girl? In the second story, why is the boy reduced to stealing? In the third story, will the boy get away? The story starters leave **lots of questions hanging in the air, so that the reader wants to read on to find out what happens next**. That is what you have to do when you begin your own story.

Strategies for story starters

Here are some ideas to help you to get started.

- Start your stories with a bang – do not wander into the story with lots of details that can emerge as the story unfolds – start the action straight away!

- Make sure you **introduce some sort of question,** so the reader wants to find out more.

- Make sure that right from the beginning you use wonderful, descriptive vocabulary. It helps to set the scene.

- Concentrate hard on the beginning of your story – it is worth writing a couple of sentences in rough to make sure you can re-draft and change your work, making it as exciting as you can.

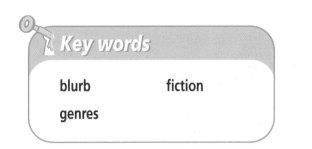

Mum always says, 'Don't tell stories!'

I'm sure she wouldn't mind if you actually did some homework, though!

Have a go...

*Choose ten **fiction** books off the shelves – they could be from home, at school or in the library. Look at the first paragraph of each story. Do they all have a question that needs answering? How does the author create tension or excitement?*

Key words

blurb	fiction
genres	

Quick Test

Choose one of these titles and write your own story starter – just the first paragraph.

- The Creature in the Darkness
- The Runaway
- A Horse Washed by Moonlight
- Friend or Foe?

Story writing process 2

Clustering ideas

When writers are going to write a story, they often have lots of ideas before they start. They often make notes to help them, perhaps in a notebook, or more likely these days on their computer!

One way to make notes is **clustering**.

Clustering means making a collection of ideas, jotted down on paper. Choose a word that describes your main subject – then let your mind wander! Write down any words that come into your head around the word. The ideas do not have to be written in full sentences – they can just be words or phrases written down as they come to you. Draw lines and arrows between words and ideas that seem to be connected and that will help your trains of thought to develop.

Useful words: sparks, licking flames, glittering, explosion

girl thinks she sees him when a fire starts at her house

school /welfare services become involved

parents begin to suspect she is setting fires herself – an arsonist?

no one believes her – she sees the demon elsewhere – puts out fires in bins, etc.

troublesome creature – tries to start fires maliciously

Top Tip

When you take your SATs at school, you will need to plan your story. Learning how to use clustering will help you to get your ideas in order. It is a useful thing to do when writing non-fiction too, as it helps you to think your ideas through really carefully.

Get lots of practice

Try to do lots of clustering to get some practice. Try planning an article for your school **newsletter**, if you have one. But planning stories is perhaps the best – because you can let your imagination run wild!

Here are some ideas for stories for you – try clustering for these titles, and then choose your favourite and write the story!

- The Dragon in the Cellar – you find a small dragon in the coal pile, which is getting smaller, because people do not believe in dragons any more.

- Unwanted! Feral Cat Colony – life and battles amongst a colony of wild cats that no one wants, living on a rubbish tip in a big city.

- My Brother's a Vampire! You make a really weird discovery one night. You knew your brother was mean, but…!

- Emergency at the Stables – a horse is injured and you are the only one who can get help!

My brother's a vampire? That sounds like the kind of story I could believe!

And I could enjoy!

Have a go...

Keep a notebook or a file on the computer for story ideas. Authors use these all the time. They may go back to ideas they wrote years ago to write a new story!

Key words

SATs

Quick Test

Try clustering to plan a story about a new family that comes to live in your street. They only come out at night. They are all very pale, and only wear black…

Story writing process 3

Why are characters important?

Think about the best stories you have ever read. What do you remember about them? It is probably the **characters**!

Great characters:

Joe Pipkin (in *The Halloween Tree* by Ray Bradbury) – lively, wild and fun.

Lirael (in *Abhorsen* by Garth Nix) – courageous, imaginative and fierce.

Hermione (in the *Harry Potter* books by J.K. Rowling) – brave, intelligent and good at solving problems.

Mary (in *Witch Child* by Celia Rees) – enduring, strong and intelligent.

Amon the cat (in *The Cats of Seroster* by Robert Westall) – wise, loyal, and 'faithful beyond death'.

Lyra (from *His Dark Materials* by Philip Pullman) – resourceful, brave and imaginative.

Characters are the most important part of any story. If a character feels real, the reader will care about what happens to them – and will want to read more! However exciting the action is, if the reader does not care about the characters, they will get bored.

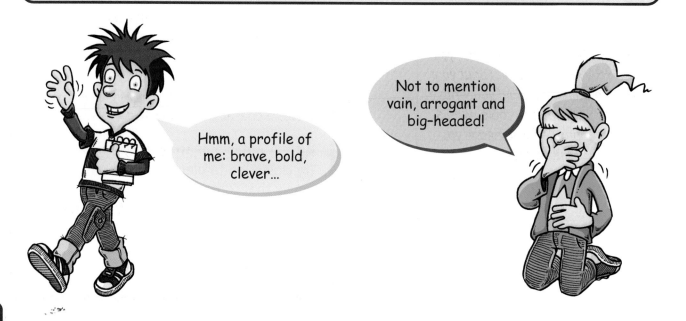

Hmm, a profile of me: brave, bold, clever...

Not to mention vain, arrogant and big-headed!

Character profiling

Beware of writing 'cardboard characters'! That means characters who are not much more than a name. In a really good story, characters are fleshed out and made real. Not an easy task!

That is where character profiling comes in. When you are planning a story, you need to really think about the characters – not just what they look like, but how they feel and how this affects their actions and **motives**.

Character profiling is drawing a picture in words of the person you are describing. To help you to write a profile, ask yourself these questions:

What is the main reason for this character to appear in the story? If they have a task to do, perhaps you can make them strong-willed and full of purpose.

If the character is a villain, do they have any redeeming features (things that make them seem a little less wicked – love for a person or animal, or a reason in their past for why they act so badly)?

If the character is a hero, is there something they could do that is less than perfect – to make them a bit more human?

Try to **'get inside' your characters**. Imagine being the character – how would they walk? Make the way you describe your character show the sort of person he or she is. If she is fierce, she could 'stride'. If he is timid, he could scuttle or creep. **Show** the reader what the character is like, **rather than just telling** them she is fierce/he is timid.

How does the character talk? Imagine them saying something. Do they speak with confidence or are they shy?

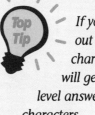

If you write a story for a test, sketch out a quick description of your main character. Creating a 'real' character will get you the highest marks. A high level answer will have well 'drawn' characters.

Have a go...

After you have read a book that you have really enjoyed, think about your favourite character. Could you write a profile for them? You could write a character profile for someone you know, too!

Key words

motives

Quick Test

Write a character profile for:

1. A girl in a mystery story.
2. A bully.
3. A very old, incredibly wise person.
4. A teenage witch.
5. A wrestler.

Story writing process 4

Creating a plot

It would be lovely if everyone was so great at writing stories that all they had to do was pick up a pen and let their creative genius flow. In the real world, though, we have to **rely on things to help us along** – like story plans. Story plans can be simple; some just ask you to think about the **beginning, middle and end** of your story. Others are more complicated and ask you to answer a series of questions.

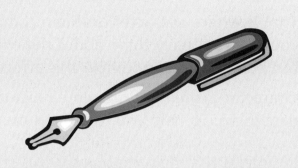

Whichever type of story plan you use, it will help you to think about your story in detail before you start to write. In your KS2 SATs, you will be given a chance to **quickly plan out your story**. The more you know about story-planning in advance, the easier it will be.

Questions to ask yourself

When you are planning a story, ask yourself these questions:

- Where does your story begin?

- Does the story setting help to build **atmosphere**? (If it is a ghost story, is the story set in a spooky place, for example?)

- Who is going to appear in your story? Do you have a main character? Are there any heroes or villains?

- Have you thought of a gripping beginning to hook your reader, so that they want to read more?

- How does the story develop? Are there any major changes or surprises during the story?

- Have you done a character profile?

- Have you thought of a good, strong ending? Is there a twist in the tale (something unexpected at the end)?

Have a go...

Look at endings – how do writers make sure they write a good, strong ending? Short story collections are a good place to look.

Top Tip *The more practice you get at writing story plans, the better. Being able to plan a story quickly will mean you have more time to write – and pick up maximum marks!*

Key words

atmosphere

Quick Test

Take the ideas you wrote for page 79 about the strange new family that have come to live in your street, and write a story plan using the questions above. You may even like to write the story!

Story writing process 5

Final draft

You are going to test your skills as an author now – from plan to final draft!

- Clustering
- Story plan
- Character profile
- Story starter
- Strong ending

Your choice of titles is:

- Beyond the Sea
- Starcat
- Day of the Spiders
- Golden Summer

You can decide to make your story from any genre you want – romance, science fiction, horror – you choose!

Top Tip
*When you are given a story title, identify the key words, e.g. An Awful Day. Key words give strong clues about the kind of writing wanted. Try listing **synonyms** of the key words (e.g. horrible, dreadful) and use this vocabulary in your story.*

I'm writing a story about a girl who gets eaten by spiders – and she looks just like Mel!

I'm writing a horror story – it's about Sam's eating habits!

Stage One

Clustering – remember to jot down all of your ideas and exciting vocabulary.

Story plan – check page 83 to remind yourself of the questions you need to ask.

Character profile – make your characters real, so the reader cares about what happens to them.

Stage Two

Story starter – think of an exciting way to hook your readers, to make them want to find out more.

Think of a problem to be solved.

Story ending – make sure your story **does not just fizzle out** – 'and then they had their tea/went to bed'. Make it interesting!

Stage Three

This is the 'editing' stage. Could you use more interesting words? Does your story make sense?

Only at the end should you worry about spelling, punctuation, etc. If you worry as you write, it will spoil the flow!

Have a go...

Read as many stories as you can – it is the best way to learn the craft of writing.

Key words

synonyms

Quick Test

Write a story without using a plan, then write one using a planning framework. Which did you find easier? Why did you choose that method?

Poetry

Wonderful words

Poetry is a great source of **descriptive and wonderful words**. Look at the examples below.

Top Tip *Try to read a variety of poems. Look for poetry collections in the library at school. The more you read them, the easier it is to write them.*

Kennings

Kennings are a way of describing things without actually saying what they are. A poem can be made by making a list of kennings.

Read this poem and try to guess what it is about!

Face-slapper
Finger-pincher
Frost-painter
Snow-bringer
Water-freezer

Guessed yet? It is about winter!

Now write your own kennings poem. You could make a booklet with your poem on one side and what it is about on the right-hand side under a flap, so people have to guess!

I'm going to write a kenning about football: crowd-thriller, scarf-flutterer...

I'm going to write a kenning about Sam: sister-botherer, sweet-stealer...

List poems

A **list poem** is just what it says – a list! You could write a colour poem as a list.

Yellow is… a ripe banana, a juicy lemon, the warmth of the sun.

Blue is… the summer sea, the sky at midday, a robin's egg.

Green is… a glistening tree frog, a fresh spring leaf, a grasshopper's wings.

Red is… a glowing sunset, a ladybird's back, a silken poppy petal.

Now write your own list poem. You could write it about the seasons or even the months of the year. You could write your lists on season shapes (such as: spring – a lamb, summer – a sun, autumn – a leaf, winter – a snowman) and make a mobile for your room.

Have a go...

Look at the man in the moon poetry site – lots of great ideas to have a go at! http://maninthemoon.co.uk/

Key words

kennings

Quick Test

1 Make up a list poem and a kenning about summer. Read them both out loud to yourself – or an audience, if you are feeling brave! Which poem do you prefer, and why?

National Test practice

Writing a story

You are going to write a story. By the time you take your SATs, you will be an expert!

You can decide to make your story any genre you want – romance, science fiction, horror – you choose!

Remember to follow these stages:

- Make a plan, such as clustering your ideas. Jot down notes and any exciting vocabulary that springs to mind.

- Story plan – check pages 82–83 to remind yourself of the questions you need to ask.

- Character profile – make your characters lifelike, so the reader cares about what happens to them.

- Story ending – make sure your story does not just fizzle out – 'and then they had their tea/went to bed'… Make it exciting!

Choose from one of these story starters.

The mist swirled round her, like dead white fingers pulling at her ankles. She shuddered as she thought of the task that lay before her.

"What do you mean, stupid?" grumbled Macy. "I think after what you've just suggested, you're the stupid one!"

The sun glittered on the water, like millions of shards of glass. The boy stared out to sea, wondering how long he would have to wait.

The grey rain trickled down the car window. Gemma listened as the wipers swished rhythmically. She felt as miserable as the weather.

Top Tip

Do not forget to read through your story to make sure it makes sense and that you do not flip backwards and forwards with tenses – easy when you are in a rush!

Comprehension

Read the passage below and answer the questions.

Eleanor dangled her suntanned arm out of the car window as her mother drove across the purple and green patchwork moors. She leant her head against the headrest, closing her eyes. The sun was warming her skin, and she breathed in the spicy smell of the heather with a sigh of pleasure.

"Look, Eleanor!" Eleanor's mum Isobel pulled the car into a viewing point. She pointed to a dark shape gliding above the moor, its splayed wing feathers looking like fat brown fingers. "It's a buzzard! Do you know, for a long time, people thought that those magnificent birds killed lambs. So many were shot that they nearly died out. I read that the numbers were on the increase. What a grand sight!"

Her dark eyes sparkled. Eleanor smiled fondly at her mum. She loved the countryside and all the creatures in it. She started the engine up again, driving slowly and carefully on the winding road. They were on their way home. Eleanor's face glowed with excitement as she thought of the animals she would see that morning. She had been to visit her godmother, Hilary, and had missed all her pets. Eleanor adored Moss and Bramble, the sheepdogs, with their bright eyes that glittered with intelligence, and the way that the horses blew their warm, musky breath on her hand as she gave them carrots.

As they pulled into the yard, they saw Eleanor's dad, Kevin. He looked a little anxious.

"Hi, girls! Have a good time?" he asked. "Now, don't be worried, but Sweetpea has a nasty cut on her leg. The greedy thing escaped from her pen and was rooting about in the rubbish when she cut herself on a piece of broken glass. The cut is very deep, Isobel. I bathed it carefully in antiseptic, and covered the cut with a gauze pad. I'm not sure if she needs a vet."

"Oh, no! Let's take a look at her," said Isobel. The animals on the smallholding were mainly hers. She always worried about them when she was away from home. Eleanor scrambled out of the car and loped after her dad towards the goat shed. As they entered the shed, Eleanor was greeted by the warm, sweet smell of fresh hay wafting through the air. Sweetpea, an Angora goat, bleated pitifully and tried shakily to stand up. Isobel stroked the goat's soft, woolly flank and murmured soothingly to her. She examined the goat's leg quickly and efficiently, then turned to Eleanor.

"Could you fetch my first aid kit from the car, Eleanor?"

Eleanor slid off the straw bale she had chosen as a seat, the stalks tickling her legs as she moved. She scooted out of the door of the shed, running across the cobbled farmyard to the car. Soon she was back, clutching the kit.

"What a good helper you are," smiled Kevin. "I don't know how I've managed here without you!"

Eleanor smiled at her dad and stroked Sweetpea's head.

"I've put a few closure strips on the wound. Sweetpea will be just fine in a few days – I think it looked worse than it really was," said Isobel. "She'll soon be back out there, chasing Gracie!" Gracie was their other goat, a Toggenburg.

Eleanor smiled at her mum and ran out into the sunshine. She walked slowly up to the old barn, now a tea room, and her tummy growled as she saw the slices of home-baked cakes lined up on the bright counter. Mrs. Cooper, her gran, looked up as she spooned cream onto a strawberry scone.

"Hello, sweetheart! Do you know, I made far too many syrup flapjacks this morning. I wonder if you know anyone who could take some off my hands?"

Eleanor's face split in an enormous grin.

"You must have heard my tummy growling!" she said. "Can I take one for Alex and Beth too, please?"

Mrs. Cooper wrapped two crumbly flapjacks in a flowery napkin and gave them to Eleanor. The thick, syrupy smell made her mouth water.

"Thanks, Grandma!" she cried happily as she ran off in search of her brother and sister.

Don't forget:

Skimming, scanning and key words (see pages 32–33).

Questions

1 What bird do Eleanor and her mother see on the moors?

_____

2 Where had Eleanor been?

_____

3 Why does Kevin look anxious as Eleanor and Isobel enter the farmyard?

_____

_____

4 What breed of goat is Sweetpea?

_____

5 Who is Gracie?

_____

6 How does Isobel treat Sweetpea's injury?

_____

_____

7 Who is Mrs. Cooper?

_____

8 What had Mrs. Cooper been doing that morning?

_____

_____

9 What are Eleanor's brother and sister called?

_____

10 How do we know that Eleanor loves animals?

_____

_____

_____

_____

Answers

Speaking and listening

PAGES 4–5 TALKING AND READING ALOUD

1 to help you to listen to ideas, to organise your thoughts to make speeches, to speak effectively and to be persuasive
2 if you can explain things well, people will understand your ideas
3 pretend to yourself that your tongue has become very heavy
4 a report on a suitable subject such as your hobby or pet
5 practise reading aloud to your family

PAGES 6–7 DEBATING

a series of notes for a speech in favour of longer lunch breaks

PAGES 10–11 TEST YOUR KNOWLEDGE

Section 1

You were told to think about these questions:

1 Is uniform more or less expensive than ordinary clothes?
   You should have compared the prices of everyday clothes and school uniform.
2 Is uniform smart – and is being smart important?
   Why should we look smart for school?

Does uniform help to make people look the same – and is that a good thing?
Does looking the same make everyone feel equal?
What do kids wear at home?
Do people tend to wear a casual uniform anyway (jeans, trainers, sweat tops, etc.)?

Section 2

You should have a for and against table, filled in with details of your research.

Section 3

You should have presented your arguments to an audience.

Reading

PAGES 12–13 READING

1 a list of what you have read today
2 a category of writing
3 a summary of the plot of a book
4 to make people want to read them; it tells the reader what the book is about
5 the artwork on the cover, the illustrations inside the book, the blurb, if they like the author's work

PAGES 14–15 READING BETWEEN THE LINES

1 looking beyond the obvious meaning of words
2 any appropriate answer giving an example of a book with a message or hidden meaning

PAGES 16–17 WHAT MAKES A 'GOOD READ'?

1 the fact that you have enjoyed the book; whether you found the book's subject interesting
2 a good strong story line, an exciting beginning, a strong – and even surprising – ending, believable, realistic characters

PAGES 18–19 FICTION AND NON-FICTION

1 any three of: fast, flowing text, you read it from the beginning to end, very personal style, not usually illustrated for older readers, new words can be worked out from the story
2 any three of: you can dip into it, lots of illustrations, specialised vocabulary, has a glossary, impersonal author style, skimmed then relevent section re-read later
3 a dictionary of specialised vocabulary
4 reading through quickly, to find information

5 fiction – non-fiction is dipped into in order to find information

PAGES 20–21 AUTHORS AND NARRATORS

1 writes a piece of work
2 a storyteller
3 the person who wrote the book; the narrator is the 'person' in the book who tells the story
4 the story of the author's life
5 yes – an author often narrates a story him or herself

PAGES 22–23 DESCRIPTION AND IMAGERY

1 describes something by saying it is like something else
2 describes something by saying it actually IS something else
3 gives human characteristics to things that are not human

PAGES 24–25 ONOMATOPOEIA AND ALLITERATION

1 drip, squash, splash, pop
2 sipped, grabbed, ten
3 where the consonant sounds in words are repeated
4 where the vowel sounds in words are repeated

PAGES 26–27 AMBIGUITY

1 Because it was hungry, the hedgehog ate the slug.
2 Because it was naughty, the cat chased the hamster.
3 Because the cat was lost, the girl picked it up.
4 Because the boy was nasty, he laughed at the crying baby.

PAGES 28–29 SPECIAL WORDS

1 the unique reference number of a book

2 additional information to explain difficult words and is found at the bottom of a page
3 a collection of extra information added at the end of a book
4 words that are added in brackets to a piece of writing to give us more information; sometimes words in parenthesis are explanations, or they may be afterthoughts
5 a collection of useful words and their meanings

PAGES 30–31 LIFE STORIES

1 a book about your own life
2 a book about someone else's life
3 Curriculum Vitae
4 when applying for jobs
5 an appropriate CV should have been written

PAGES 32–33 COMPREHENSION SKILLS

1 reading through a passage quickly to find out what it is about
2 words that answer important questions
3 to look for key words
4 understanding
5 whether you have understood what you have read

PAGES 36–37 TEST YOUR KNOWLEDGE

Section 1

1 Link
2 an evil wizard
3 to take control of the Tri force – the source of ultimate power
4 Power, Wisdom and Bravery.
5 it will split into three parts

Section 2
1 1348
2 men, young and strong
3 carried sponges soaked in vinegar, and posies of flowers called 'tussie-mussies' to ward off the plague fumes
4 fleas on rats
5 sneezing – a symptom of the plague – and dying

Writing

PAGES 38–39 CLAUSES
1 a single clause with a subject and a verb
2 a part of a sentence with a subject and a verb
3 a sentence with more than one clause
4 a sentence with two important clauses

PAGES 40–41 CONTRACTIONS
1 won't
2 can't
3 you've
4 they're

PAGES 42–43 POSSESSIVE APOSTROPHES
1 cat's
2 girl's
3 dog's
4 boy's
5 James's

PAGES 44–45 PUNCTUATION
1 helps to make writing make sense
2 divide sentences
3 at the end of sentences, instead of a question mark or full stop
4 b

PAGES 46–47 WRITING SPEECH
1 reported speech – no speech marks
2 "I like science fiction films best," said Melanie.
3 "Would you like a sweet?" asked Bethany.
4 reported speech – no speech marks
5 "I hate cold weather," said Eleanor, "but I love the snow."

PAGES 48–49 PLURALS
1 dogs
2 pianos
3 calves
4 babies
5 potatoes

PAGES 50–51 NOUNS
1 proper
2 common
3 collective
4 common
5 common

PAGES 52–53 VERBS
1 P 2 A 3 P 4 A 5 A

PAGES 54–55 ADJECTIVES
many answers are possible, for instance:
1 fluffy, juicy
2 terrifying, crumbling
3 delicious, yellow
4 enormous, glistening
5 sunny, beautiful

PAGES 56–57 CLICHÉS
1 over-used words and phrases
2 common phrases that should not be taken literally
3 a Her grandad lets her have her own way.
   b He likes things one minute and not the next.
   c Don't tell anyone.
   d He always thinks of something.

PAGES 58–59 EXCITING VOCABULARY
1 shout, call, reply, whisper
2 stride, step, saunter, march
3 gobble, taste, consume, munch
4 leap, bounce, pounce
5 snooze, dream, doze

PAGES 60–61 WRITERS CREATING MOODS
animosity, insulting, jeering, sneered, bellowed

PAGES 62–63 HOW ENGLISH IS ENGLISH?
1 Hindi
2 Hindi/Urdu
3 Hindi
4 Arabic
5 Hindi

PAGES 64–65 DRAMA
an appropriate profile of a character from a film, with details about the way the character talks, looks etc.

PAGES 66–67 WRITING INSTRUCTIONS
1 Don't be silly!
2 No smoking.
3 No diving.
4 Take 250g of chocolate.
5 Fix the paper together with tape.

PAGES 68–69 PERSUASIVE WRITING
a well produced finished leaflet, showing evidence of persuasive language

PAGES 70–71 WRITING A REPORT
a tree diagram planning a report of a day out

PAGES 72–73 WRITING A RECOUNT
a timeline and a piece of biographical writing about your chosen person

PAGES 74–75 IMPROVING YOUR WRITING SKILLS
any completed piece of writing – and evidence of the stages involved in creating the piece, such as research, planning sheets, etc

PAGES 76–77 GETTING STARTED WITH STORIES
any story starter using the titles given; should be exciting and set the scene so the reader wants to read on

PAGES 78–79 CLUSTERING
a cluster of ideas that develops the idea given – a pale family that only comes out at night

PAGES 80–81 CHARACTERS
a character profile that gives details about each of the characters listed; should give details about the personality of the characters as well as the physical appearance

PAGES 82–83 PLOTTING
The ideas on the story cluster (p78-79) should now be worked up into a plan – what will happen during the story? How will the story develop? How will it end?

PAGES 84–85 WRITING THE STORY
two stories (one written with a plan; one without) to compare – which was easier to write?

PAGES 86–87 POETRY
two poems – a kenning and a list poem – that describe 'Summer'. A brief explanation about which poem was preferred, and why

National Test practice

WRITING A STORY
a story planned and written to fit the given theme

COMPREHENSION
1 a buzzard
2 visiting her godmother, Hilary
3 because Sweetpea, the goat, has cut her leg quite badly
4 an Angora goat
5 a Toggenburg goat
6 Isobel puts closure strips on the wound
7 Eleanor's grandma
8 baking flapjacks
9 Alex and Beth
10 from the words, 'Eleanor's face glowed with excitement as she thought of the animals she would see that morning.' We are also told that she missed her pets whilst she was away.

Glossary

active verb where the subject does the action, e.g. the cat scratched the boy

adjective a word that describes a noun

alliteration when a sound is repeated in a sentence

ambiguity when the meaning of a sentence is unclear

apostrophe punctuation used to show a letter has been missed out, or that something belongs to somebody

appendix a collection of extra information added at the end of a book

assonance where vowel sounds are repeated

atmosphere mood, setting

author the person who wrote something

autobiography the story of a person's life, written by themselves

biography the story of a person's life, written by someone else

blurb information given on the back of a book – often a short synopsis of part of the story

book review a written response to a book, describing what happens in it, how you felt about it and whether you would recommend it to others

characteristics things that identify a character – looks, actions, walk, voice, etc.

chronologically in the order something happened

clause a part of a sentence. It has a subject and a verb. It is not a sentence and does not have to start with a capital letter, or end with a full stop

clichés words and phrases that have been used so many times that people get over-familiar – and bored – with them!

collective noun a singular name for a group of things, e.g. herd

common noun a word that gives the name of a type of thing, e.g. dog, house, person

complex sentence built around a main clause and also has less important clauses

compound sentence two important clauses; each clause would make a simple sentence on its own, but can be joined to make a compound sentence

comprehension exercise an exercise that tests to see how much you have understood about a passage you have been asked to read

conclusion the final part of a piece of writing

contractions words that have letters missing; an apostrophe shows where the letters have been missed out

Curriculum Vitae (CV) a record of work, interests and education that people use when they are applying for work

debate a reasoned argument between two teams of people

devise (drama) to create or 'make up' a piece of work to be performed

dialogue when characters talk to each other and speech marks are used to show this

facts things that are true and provable

fiction made-up stories and writing

footnotes notes at the bottom of a page that add extra explanations or information

formal writing writing such as reports or formal letters

genre horror, romance, science fiction – these are all genres

glossary a collection of useful words and their meanings

hot seating (drama) where a person answers questions in character to help them to understand the character they are playing

idiom a common phrase that is used and understood – but should not be taken literally!

imagery ways of making 'word pictures' – such as similes and metaphors

index an alphabetical list of contents in a book that helps the reader to find particular subjects

informal (writing) writing to friends, etc.

ISBN number on the back of a book used to catalogue or order it

jargon language or vocabulary peculiar to a particular group

kennings a way of describing things without naming them

loanwords words taken directly from languages other than the one spoken

main clause the most important part of the sentence, containing the main idea; would make sense on its own

metaphors ways of describing something by saying it *is* something else, e.g. the moon *was* a tennis ball

mnemonic making silly sentences or words to help you to remember things

motives why someone, such as a character in a novel, does something or acts in a certain way

narrator the storyteller

National Tests See SATs

non-fiction factual writing such as found in a newspaper

noun a naming word – places, people, things

onomatopoeia a word that sounds like the thing it is describing, e.g. crash, bang

opinion what one person or a group of people thinks or believes

parenthesis words that are added in brackets to a piece of writing to give us more information; words in parenthesis are often explanations, or afterthoughts

passive verb where the object does the action, e.g. the boy was scratched by the cat

personification when something is described by giving it human characteristics

plural more than one

possessive apostrophe shows that something belongs to somebody or something

proofread re-reading a piece of writing to check it makes sense, has no errors, etc.

proper noun the name of a person or place, e.g. Mark, France

pronoun a word used in place of a noun e.g. *I*, *you*, *he*, *this*, *who*, *what*

punctuation marks such as ' , ! ? which are used to make meaning clear

quotation a sentence or passage copied from a piece of work, exactly as it was first written or taken down exactly as it was first said

report a piece of non-fiction writing that presents information about a subject

reported speech when someone tells us about what someone has said, rather than a person actually speaking

SATs Standard Assessment Tests (also known as National Tests). In primary school, SATs are carried out at the end of Key Stage One (at age 7) and at the end of Key Stage Two (at age 11). Tests are taken in English, Maths and Science

sequel a book written to continue the story begun in a previous book

similes descriptions that say something is like something else – 'The sun was like an orange balloon'

simple sentence a sentence with one clause: The cat was grey.

speaking and listening A skill described in the National Curriculum as important for pupils to learn. It means being able to listen to ideas and comment on them. It can also mean giving a speech, oral report or taking part in a debate.

speech marks " " punctuation marks that show direct speech is being used

subordinate clause the less important clause in a sentence; they do not make a sentence by themselves

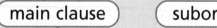

main clause   subordinate clause

Helen ran quickly, because she saw the ice-cream van.

synonyms words that have nearly the same meanings

tense when something happens: kicked – past tense, kicks/kicking – present tense, shall kick – future tense

thesaurus a collection of words organised according to meaning, i.e. big: huge, large, massive

trilogy a set of three books (films and plays)

verb an action or doing word

viewpoint from a particular character's way of looking at things

vocabulary the words of a language

voice who is telling the story